Contemporary American Poetry
78 New Poems

Contemporary American Poetry
78 New Poems

An Eagle Falcon Publication

By
Dalward J DeBruzzi

E-BookTime, LLC
Montgomery, Alabama

Contemporary American Poetry
78 New Poems

Copyright © 2018 by Dalward J DeBruzzi

All rights reserved. No part of this book may be reproduced or transmitted in any form or by any means, electronic or mechanical, including photocopying, recording, or by any information storage and retrieval system, without permission in writing from the copyright owner.

Library of Congress Control Number: 2018937290

ISBN: 978-1-60862-725-7

First Edition
Published March 2018
E-BookTime, LLC
6598 Pumpkin Road
Montgomery, AL 36108
www.e-booktime.com

Contents

A Credo 9
A Valentines Tale 10
Beauty 12
Buddies 14
Can I Improve? 16
Captured 17
Cares 18
Chickie Me 19
Cold Reality 21
Country Honor Respect 23
Crystallizing Dreams 25
Disappointed But No Regrets 27
Don't You Wish You Were Me? 29
Eternal Crucible 30
Etiquette 32
Father Knew Best 34
Forever 36
Golden Memories 37
Greed Is Toxic 38
Human Sensitivity 40
I Passed 42
Ill Prepared 44
Invulnerable 46
Is Death Feared By All? 48

Contents

Is it Psychosomatic? 49
It's Always Been Unknown 51
Journey Endless 52
Just a Cow 53
Light Traffic 55
Lucky 57
Microcosm-Nature-Cosmos 59
Missed 60
Motives? 62
Mr. Solar 63
Mr. Wind 65
Mumbo Jumbo Tumbo 66
My Daughter 68
My Good Deed 70
My Orchards 72
My Regret 74
My Ship 75
My Vicarious Travels 77
Our Ole Farm 78
Parting 80
Porky Piggi 82
Potent Love 84
Profound Thought 86
Proposal 87

Contents

Redemption 88
Relentless 89
Relit 90
River of Life 92
Sanctified 94
Secret Trips 95
Shades of Lilacs 96
Song Writers 98
Spells and Curses 99
The Ace 101
The Asian Miracle 102
The Dream 104
The Eelymosinarry 107
The Ferryboat 110
The Order of Life 111
The Panacea for All Ills 113
The Rose 115
Unrealistic 116
Unseen Companion 117
Unsung Brave Women 118
Vulnerable 120
Was Abortion the Right Thing? 122
What Did I Do? 124
What Is Love? 126

Contents

What Next 128
What's a Friend? 129
What's in a Name? 130
Wisdom 132
Women 134
Would This Last? 135

A Credo

Encouraged by the expressions of his lofty mind
Think the best of human kind

Yet of all the causes which fate decrees
Oft erring judgment misses by degrees

In his pure and innocent naive breast
Strict avoidance of iniquity will pass the test

His moral unblemished traits conspicuously driven
Hails his worth of character given

It's to these admirable shining souls
We pattern ourselves after, as worthy goals

by Dalward J DeBruzzi

A Valentines Tale

Am honest, keep the Sabbath am not a
  deceiver
Believe in abstinence doing right am a
  believer

My name is Barlow the butcher my life hard,
  joyless and weary
Toil from dawn to dusk at night unfulfilled
  and teary

I'm not comely, not sought by a prospective
  mate
Destined bachelorhood lonely life my likely
  fate

Paining from sorrow, Valentine's day
  tomorrow is hailed
Shop crowded with followers of cupid
  merrily regaled

Miss Frumplich a faithful frequent patron
  looked on with desire and design
Noticed same want, wish, longing in her
  eyes as mine

Contemporary American Poetry – 78 New Poems

**Customers gone confessed to each other
    with no shame
Our entwined futures now enriched from the
    line
"Will you be my valentine?"**

by Dalward J DeBruzzi

Beauty

I can love a women who is slanty eyed fair,
    brown, black
If beauty is not in lack

Love is intense passion a required initial
    ingredient
Firm character, proper, decency gentility all
    a post antecedent

I can love someone despite varied
    background
If substance steadfastness are solid,
    dignified and profound
Prospects for success will abound

This standard dismisses chances for
    destructive flaw
Although initial attraction the chemistry of
    physical draw

Contemporary American Poetry – 78 New Poems

Sexual magnetism while the original attraction
Will not survive unless substantive firm traits emerge with interaction

by Dalward J DeBruzzi

Buddies

We went through grade school high school college together
I joined the Marines our friendship did not want to sever

We served a tour in Iraq my lifelong buddy didn't make the second
Miss him with heavy heart was devastated fate cruelly beckoned

I remember fond memories of all fine times shared
Though separated in mortal terms
From the tragic loss of a friend a man learns

Though he's now in heroes heaven with saintly psychic essence
He's never away from my side or out of my presence

Though one friend mortal on earth one psychic in the beyond
Nothing thing will ever alter our eternal bond

by Dalward J DeBruzzi

Can I Improve?

Each mealtime my dinner is given to me I say
Along with prayers today

When patted on the back and on my head too
For good conduct, never sassy or rude
Attitude, fairness, honest are valued food

My head swells with pride for the accolade given
A fine reward for my motive decency driven

A child not good nor neat and clean
May miss toys and goodies to eat

Constant improvement is the object of the fray
To enhance success it might help if you pray

If all efforts fail the result desired
A sore red achy bottom may be required

by Dalward J DeBruzzi

Captured

Why oh why do you engage in squander
Your flirtatious eye that indiscriminately did
    wander

When only one can nobly claim the prize
While engaging in taunting coquetry the one
Who is captured inwardly silently cries

The light banter of tease quickens the heart
    and pulse of the stricken
Watching the light repartee induces the
    devotee to sicken

Unobtainable love kills indeed, leaves one
    in distress
Only escape is time, strong will and
    unwilling redress

by Dalward J DeBruzzi

Cares

Sun shining warmly lying on my back
Without a care or worry to distract

Gazing up at the calm placid blue sky
With puffy white clouds sailing by

Moments of contentment, no problems to wrestle
Creates a deep pleasureful sigh

These rare occasions of restful heaven
Are treasures to be cherished and leaven

Sparrows, finches, diving, climbing flinging
And winging tweeting tunes of harmonious avian singing

Exhibition lulled me to doze, drift to deep lolling encumber
Woke to silence, peace, refreshed, relaxed from restful slumber

by Dalward J DeBruzzi

Chickie Me

My name is Twiggy Chickie my confusion
    complete my feelings hurt
I was hatched in a cage, in my entire life I
    never touched dirt

My whole life was spent in a small coop,
    never left it, was fed with automatic
    food dispenser, water, never left my
    cage
I was called a pullet, told I had fine
    commercial legs on menus I would be
    a rage

Cats, dogs have organizations guarding
    their welfare,
Seeking homes for them when abandoned
    by some who dare

All I get is a bleak, aimless, unpromising
    existence
Without any means to mount resistance

With premeditated murder as my final
 inhumane atrocity
Garnishing a tasty meal for a gourmet with
 ferocity

In camouflaged finery I'm a victim who lost
 the foray
My life in jeopardy from the first day

Why? because I'm cheap, tasty and not a
 desired pet
Guilt for treatment of dogs, cats, but me
 being eaten minds are set

by Dalward J DeBruzzi

Cold Reality

Thy loveliness fastens my feasting eyes to stare
On thy bodice laces and curvature fair

Regal erect tall graceful in elegant symmetry
Rivets and commands my conquered dotage liberally

My eager fingers desire probing the delicate garments you wear
Breathe little hope to gain favor of one so fair

Entranced by stunning magnetic vision my mood bitter
My unqualified misplacement of folly exposed my necessity to be fitter

My yearning for her heartstrings distant from my orbit lost in my confusion
Were displaced in my folly and lost in delusion
Your emotions distant from my sphere and your exclusion

Contemporary American Poetry – 78 New Poems

Fertile imagination allows me to feel your
    cheek on mine
Rubbing softly as wafting caressing breezes
    envelope exquisitely fine

All visions I have is in psychic essence
My unstable yearning ends in unpleasance

One participant only expands torturous
    singular yearning
Empty hollow meaningless insensible no
    discerning

by Dalward J DeBruzzi

Country Honor Respect

I'm a patriotic veteran my heart is heavy
    befuddled confused
See fellow citizens who lost their way now
    unenthused

Cool indifferent to nation, shrines,
    institutions the pledge, the flag
    disrespected
Actions which cause people to be
    unpatriotically affected

Those who dishonor our country with
    improper forms of protest
Should surely be liable to swift arrest

If unhappy enough to engage in
    dishonorable kneeling
Visas should be applied for in new country
    more appealing

Contemporary American Poetry – 78 New Poems

Millions of people the world over pine and
yearn to join the stream of émigrés to
the USA
Their reasons are solid plenty food, drinking
water, freedom, security a job with
decent pay

Legal émigrés are welcome who honor our
culture, history, institutions and lore
Those who fail to join our national moral
fiber are not candidates of favor for
sure

by Dalward J DeBruzzi

Crystallizing Dreams

Disillusions, shattered dreams in ruins,
fractured hearts
Debris strewn wantonly in tiny parts

Fading memories of happiness, hurt,
Contentment, bliss achieved fleetingly but
all too curt

Vestiges of sorrow, nothing remains for the
morrow
Future hopes lessened brightness nothing
to borrow

Gaunt pain stricken eyes, plague, attempted
recovery of body and soul
Resurrection, introspection recovery our
primary goal

**When taints sour and vision looks dour
New hope with elan of future blooms like
beautiful flowers
Disbursing joy peace serenity from new
found powers**

by Dalward J DeBruzzi

Disappointed But No Regrets

I was a young school teacher rejected in
    divorce
I was the culprit the blameful source

Gave wife generous settlement and house
    too
So wife, son, daughter could exist in
    comfort anew

Supported children put son through college
    to career
Daughter a willing volunteer, son useless
    and insincere

Son lives in million dollar condo never a
    help no contact preferred
Without mutual respect relationship doesn't
    occur

When son married gave hundred thousand
    towards domicile
Never a hand provided or offered omission
    reviled

Dream of father and son doing a little
    something together
Never took place no connecting tether

Daughter loving and willing can't allow her
    to exert
While son is useless and is frightened of work

Destined to end in isolation alone and distant
Never cared to cause kids diversions,
    aversion consistent

Life belongs to the young their happiness I
    procure
My wish all my life was see my kids secure

Their future secure I can now gracefully
    give in
Being old, tired hard of hearing toothless,
    ready to take it on the chin

by Dalward J DeBruzzi

Contemporary American Poetry – 78 New Poems

Don't You Wish You Were Me?

Little Blackfoot, Sioux or Crow joined by
    Tata, Eskimo or Arapahoe
Little Turk, Tonk, Japanese or Hawaiian
    too!
Don't you wish that you were me?
Found tidal waves critical or annual famine
    something to avoid
Such a life may be good for you, but it's not
    as divine as mine
You may also see your diet is not as fine as
    mine
While some may eat snails, stringy meat
I eat steak, chops, chicken, ribs
You must avoid crocodiles, pythons, the
    tsetse fly, Ebola, malaria while I am
    safe and secure here at home
Oh little frigid Eskimo, arctic dweller,
    Alpiner, Saharan, Congolese, islander,
    Balanese, Tahitian, little Yemeni don't
    you wish you were me?

by Dalward J DeBruzzi

Eternal Crucible

The tintinnabulation of the cathedral bells
    were awesome in strength and power
Loud in sound and potent in spiritual
    emanation with message from its lofty
    tower

Brilliant sunshine floods the parishioners
    streaming
To their pews, seeking comforts supportive
    dogma
Immersed in ritual, prayer and communion
    dreaming

Of religion mother of order arbitrate right
    and wrong
Constrainer of wanderers who might drift in
    err ere long

Pleading noble words rise in deference and
    humility
Logic below an anchor to reason and
    tranquility

Contemporary American Poetry – 78 New Poems

**Temporal or eternal it matters not if belief
   is unyielding,
Strong and pure faith protecting and
   shielding**

by Dalward J DeBruzzi

Etiquette

Ill manners no doubt create mild or severe
    rejection
If you consume your victuals with hasty,
    careless sloppy injection

It offends the genteel upon proper reflection
Bad manners, repugnance a close connection

Amazed at some's ability to swallow food
    and drink gulp beer in surfeit
    performance
Their stomach's vast satiation generates
    stomach distress and peptic
    annoyance

Regrets when later enlarged belly, several
    chins and puffy fat
Then regret and remorse no recovery in
    store you made your choice and the
    condition is pat

Proper manners disregarded not wise, huge portions you eat with undisciplined false pride
No judgment shown when manners ignored and denied
Wiser course of action should have been tried

Bodily discharges of gases now taxed
Emissions now excessive cannot be relaxed

When the etiquette regimen ignored as a refinement
It's an annoyance and oft a peril to others in close confinement

Dining is pleasant when amidst manners with grace
It's also a way everyone can save face

by Dalward J DeBruzzi

Father Knew Best

Left the house early seeking work I try day
after day
Weeks went by no pay

Money low in house, rent coming due
Wife upset, troubled, what to do

Tramping to apply caused introspection
Recalling father's advice I had disdained
with rejection

Advised education, career then wife then
children
Failure to listen prevented proper order for
building

Cost for not complying, poor job selection
See the light attend night school with good
intention

**Trying to recover my pace and my stride to face the test
I freely concede my father knew best**

by Dalward J DeBruzzi

Forever

Oh sweet glorious married beauty when
ideally suited souls unite
With softness, dedication, tenderness, day
into night

Affectionate chains voluntarily, fastened
securely
With eagerly accepted duties, chores, no
fragility surely

Your stalwart steadfastness surpassing
your charms
Susceptibility to goodness dismissing alarms

Your collective worth profound indeed
exceeding optical pleasure
Love graven on my heart the final
comforting measure

by Dalward J DeBruzzi

Golden Memories

We'll never experience in body again
Things we once shared way back when

Deep dear memories endure forever a
    wonder cryptically known
Cannot be put asunder when affection has
    been deeply sown

Our years together, long tender and sweet
Oh my love if we could our seventy years
    repeat

As we advance to aged ripeness nearing
    ethereal residency
We pray it's together to resume our joint
    pleasantries

We plan repetition yearn for continuity as
    cosmic souls
Our desired gift immortal continuance
    together with wished preternatural
    goals

by Dalward J DeBruzzi

Greed Is Toxic

The poor struggling farmer lived a meager scant life
Ragged clothes little to eat embroiled in strife

One day in the hen coop his Rhode Island Red
Laid a shiny egg of pure gold instead

With utter delight he showed his wife how nice
Took it to town sold it for fabulous price

Each morning there after a golden egg was found
Farmer became wealthy rich fat and round

Became lazy smug spoiled declared getting up early
Too much inconvenience
Rich man like me shouldn't have to rise too soon surely can afford lenience

He reasoned kill the Rhode Island Red get
   all the eggs in one sweep
An never again will I disturb my sleep

Didn't work out the way he planned how he
   did bawl
Indolence did him in no more golden eggs at
   all

The farmer lamented his laziness and greed
Is a good example of someone who doesn't
   know when to be pleased

by Dalward J DeBruzzi

Human Sensitivity

It was early morn in the lonely deserted
    coffee house
Sitting, sipping coffee as patrons trickled in
    one by one
Man and woman came in referred to him as
    a louse

Place filled up now busy and crowded
Mixed conversation some even shouted

My morning human contact settled me for
    the day
Satisfied the human need for feeling of
    interplay

Though experience is remote fills desperate
    need
Human presence a demanding urge
    naturally decreed

Contemporary American Poetry – 78 New Poems

**Some acquire the satisfaction through
   friendship or spouse
Some through the early morning comradery
   in a coffee house**

by Dalward J DeBruzzi

I Passed

My wife is a school teacher I am an auto
parts clerk in Auto City
Everything I do I'm graded it's a pity

My house work around the house
Doing laundry, vacuuming, windows she
Awards me
An
A
She chides me that's one of the reasons I
let you stay
When a mark for wage earner is given only
uninhibited laughter is heard
But no grade

For my years of connubiality in bed graced
me with another F
Said it's all I made

Fastidious schoolies demand fine results
With effort and concentration no insults

**After decades with a personal tutor it's for me to say
The day I gave my wedding vow was my smartest play**

by Dalward J DeBruzzi

Ill Prepared

Avoided reading not one book of intricate plot
Failed to offer a mind to be got

I learned a little then forgot
Gaining and improving from learning and improving I did not

I sought love, slim, pretty, witty, younger
My eye causing yearning inspired my hunger

Though trees turn into greenery girls turn into wives
I found no motivation and discovered no drives

I see secessions of seasons with no changes in destiny or heading
Could find not a soul who would invest in me my life continued treading

As time ticked away serious scholars got the wives, jobs, careers
All I got was disappointment and tears

Contemporary American Poetry – 78 New Poems

**It's not enough to sense, feel pain, want,
yearn you must plan, prepare, pay dues
Only then success will result as all
elements of success gradually accrues**

ONLY THEN WILL YOU GET YOUR TURN!

by Dalward J DeBruzzi

Invulnerable

A small white cottage happy man and wife
Sunshine warmth contentment with life

Constantly thanking providence for their paradise
Peace, mutual sharing, trust, no unwelcome surprise

She tends to him and he to her
Doing for each other secret to rapport

Accepting duties willingly and equally we concur
Is vital to cohesive union no need to seek succor

The seasons come the seasons go
The geese fly South annually we know

Winter time brings fluffy snow
Days shorten, equinox, then the cycle begins again we know

Most things ethereal, passing through phases with strife

Except happy man and wife in small white cottage
Immune to change and alteration in their mutual dotage

by Dalward J DeBruzzi

Is Death Feared By All?

Is death a word that is feared and shunned
 by all?
By viral active young yes, with pall

By crash, drowning, terminal illness or duress
Premature ends they eagerly avoid, or
 suppress

Septuagenarian, octogenarian nonagenarian
 not so inclined,
As all applicants for rest abundant consigned

Physical systems under eroding assault,
 pain constant
Excessive immune system maligned

No peace, relief, respite from aches, age, a
 curse
Anticipate with resignation escape, a ride in
 a hearse

by Dalward J DeBruzzi

Is it Psychosomatic?

Enchanting flowers in your presence gloom
 sours
With thy glorious brightness despair and
 misery cowers

In glare of bright warmth cheer is in thee
With generous quantities of humanity

A soul may be rescued who is quite
 depressed
Even one who wanders unblessed

Expanding their brightness insulating any
 precipitous fall
A salving effect with influence aiding all

Is the flowers visual effect so strong as that?
Or is it psychosomatic or simply an
 effective form of combat
Who can judge the therapeutic effect of
 calm aura
Serenity on health and firmity
Flowers, beautiful children of mother nature
 casting joy with forceful bravura

**Mother nature's home remedy of soothing
 balm a kaleidoscope of tints shades
 with dash of a spiritual psalm
Springing from her bosom with a massive
 healing by assuaging anxieties into
 easing calm**

by Dalward J DeBruzzi

It's Always Been Unknown

Life strives for smooth placidity
Seldom fully achieved due to avidity

Desire for materiality erodes
Morality, diminished, prior to finality

There is unreliable prediction what now
    transpires
Billowing lofty paradise or raging infernos of
    fires

Labricks on Sunday cover their bets with
    generous coin, insincere contrition
Futile gestures of ineffective measures
Gaining nothing to improve position

Death is mandated for all things we decry
Accept it as natural we all live and die

by Dalward J DeBruzzi

Journey Endless

Frail fragile mortality is a permanent threat
Escaping its inevitability unlikely and unwise bet

Once I was young content happy sprightly and blooming
Misfortune from wayside time methodical marching on ghostly looming

Decrepitation closed in from time's savage assault
Steady trail to deterioration by ethereal fault

Time's merciless charge determined to achieve inquest
Time is a deadly foe plodding patient never in jest

In recollection of youthful exuberance when living was bright with delight
Furthest thought way down road conclusion looming

by Dalward J DeBruzzi

Just a Cow

Every one pets a dog or horse no one ever pets me
You'll change your view when I clue you in you see

I am who they need when they want milk, cheese,
Malted milks or veal
My disappearance would be a loss you people would feel

It's not a smart idea to invite an ordeal
Some respect is a small appeal

No more baby food vitamin A, boots, shoes, vests,
Cowhides my absence would be missing lost treasure
Loss of live giving food, jobs would be the measure

Creameries, bottling plants, farmers,
drivers, just a few who owe their
employment to me
I crave not adulation but seek due
appreciation I decree

Movie stars, football, baseball, basketball
players give entertainment to amuse their
fans with revelry
I give nourishment for life health and
longevity

You now are reminded I deserve
glorification not depreciation

by Dalward J DeBruzzi

Light Traffic

I live on a farm in the Midwest
Living in rural area is the best

Fewer people, less congestion and tension
Know everyone, like a well knit family
    extension

After dark one night my girl and I drove off
    to attend a concert
We whisked through town, around the bend
Turned a corner came to road's end

On the lonely stretch of road a railroad
    crossing gate came down banging
Lowered with flashing lights bells, clanging

As the malevolent train impacted with
    destructive force
We missed the concert now irrelevant of
    course

We still love music with all its pleasing rings
An even mastered plucking the harp strings

**Even less road congestion no insurance an accident will not occur vigilance is required
Odds and luck may conspire to send unlucky victims to be prematurely expired**

by Dalward J DeBruzzi

Lucky

I'm average looking, have an average job
    only went as far as high school

Don't dress snappy, use drugs or drink
    alcohol
Don't catch girl's notice not impressive at
    all

Only chance find girl who can see me and
    agree
A full true heart with faithful love will suit
    thee

I possess no wealth not a dapper dresser
    but found a maiden containing inner
    treasure
Loyalty, true, faithful, satisfied with simple
    pleasure

Her declaration to me of dedicated love for
    all time, all ages providential
    handsome wages
Encouraged me to swear my fidelity to her
    before the sages

To find my compatible mate took long
   agonized search
My luck was fortuitous and blessed
I found an ideal maiden worthy to be
   addressed

by Dalward J DeBruzzi

Microcosm-Nature-Cosmos

When daylight hours are done and over
With rotation away from revolving sun
In darkness does all mortality deceivingly pause?
The disappearing rays lower, people withdraw in awe
As the blending shadows emerge in force
Crops, flowers people seem mortal and vanish
It's only an illusion not a permanent banishing
When blackness of night edges to dissipation
Mortality resumes with solar restoration

by Dalward J DeBruzzi

Missed

As a mortal you bowed and deserted me so abrupt
True felt the loss deeply but unaware feelings corrupt

How could my vision and heart be immune and unaware
Not knowing the depth of my pain and despair

How can I claim normal vision and yet be so blind
The omission or lapse is inexcusable unkind

Forgetting you less than a minute was unforgivable
Yet my guilt earned though detested not livable

As I reflect late in my life you were by far my biggest loss I dejectedly abhor
Now knowing the severity of pain could just once your heavenly face effect restore

Contemporary American Poetry – 78 New Poems

The worst jolt and severe wrench to suffer
   above all
Is to relive over and over with frequent
   recall

Reversal of misfortune beyond measure
Hopefully can recoup my infirm faith despite
   displeasure

by Dalward J DeBruzzi

Motives?

We met, we dated we got involved
We had problems they were resolved

She was agreeable, deferred to me in every way
Endless reasons to be coveted today

Sweetness, apparently a jewel to be admired
So delectable she was never tired

Kind, natural, voluptuous, she adored my relatives, my folks, everything seemed to be perfection
Judgment excellent as a selection

Family, friends enthusiastic, no reason to delay idyllic euphoristic expectation of connubial rapture
With the one whose heart I was lucky to capture

by Dalward J DeBruzzi

Mr. Solar

My name is Mr. Solar known as the sun
My life and duties are anything but fun

I flood the earth with warmth and energy
Providing the elements with required synergy

I am creator of billions of flowers on the planet earth
Flood them with life giving rays from birth nurtured anon
A credit to me I have never picked one

I feel I am noble, generous, but must complain and gripe
No one cares to marry me saying I'm not their type

They say I'm not pretty, have no shape or form
Only emotion exhibited toward me as suitor is scorn

Contemporary American Poetry – 78 New Poems

Well if I am destined to be celibate I could care less
My life giving rays earn me plaudits and reknown

My good work sates my psyche satisfies my cosmic soul
With eons to go I'll keep doing my duty, life giving, to all, my sworn goal

by Dalward J DeBruzzi

Mr. Wind

Watched you fling kites hither and yon
Up and down, low and high
Contesting birds their passage way by gusts
and currents impediments to stay

I see your effects from the things you brew
But never have seen you when you do

You're mysterious and secret always,
incognito
In currents or drafts your energy infinito

You're active and roaring all day,
sometimes at night
Heard with disturbing fright

Your screeching cries, thrashing branches,
sighs, crashing thunder
On dark lonely nights destroy slumber

by Dalward J DeBruzzi

Mumbo Jumbo Tumbo

Lived in a thatch hut in Congo
Went out every day to forage for food
Not daring today or in an anxious mood

Some days were good and some days bad
Coming home empty handed remorseful and sad

They hefted their spears trekked up on prey

The boys decided to avoid baboons crocs
Monkeys, hippos, elephants nothing large
Decided to seek and hunt bird flocks
A bushbuck or an antelope nothing that will charge

Bushbucks gbeles nestling turtles to be found
Chances thinning out
Maybe a buffalo or antelope to run to ground
Bagged a gazelle two nestling turtles caught out

Contemporary American Poetry – 78 New Poems

**Three boys return triumphantly to their
home and village
Now filled with fresh food
Lucky for them they were able to pillage
Family happy all in fine mood.**

by Dalward J DeBruzzi

My Daughter

My daughter is a kind sweet loving girl
    never pleaded
Helped me over the years with everything I
    needed

Always offers to help me any way she could
Had to decline to over tax her would be a
    crime

She's a willing helper offers constant
    assistance
Felt guilty can't allow her to spread herself
    thin offered resistance

Love her dearly, miss her with passion
Getting your way not always in fashion

I am proud of her concern, frugality,
    common sense
Her delightful aid she will freely dispense

She tends to mother with tender care and
    feeling
Pampers us with comforts appealing

We both begged forgive us for times did scold
It was done to teach right way and to mold

by Dalward J DeBruzzi

My Good Deed

The crying little child sniffling in the misty rain
Lost or abandoned it's the same

Tell me little darlin what happened to you please
Together we will dry your tears, fear will cease

Were you hurt in any way by someone you knew
Oh my little darlin tell me and I will surely help you

Here come sit upon my knee cry yourself dry from all your flowing tears
Then we'll solve your dilemma and banish your fears

Contemporary American Poetry – 78 New Poems

**Rain has lifted, mommy appears frantic on
    the scene most contrite
Tiny child relieved happy hugs 'n kisses both
Mommy and me in delight
Now shed of great fear and fright**

by Dalward J DeBruzzi

My Orchards

When the apples are juicy red the harvest
    on time
Yield is abundant everything is fine

Branches limber, flexible bending with
    apples at last
Serving pickers as they reach near and far
    to grasp

Peaches look ripe golden savory tempting
    taste buds with delight to the eye
Their color tantalizing mouth watering juicy,
    sliced or warm tasty pie

Rich bluish plums glorious in their tints and
    tight skins
Their tasty tangy pulp stimulating to taste
    buds no whims

Contemporary American Poetry – 78 New Poems

Housewives eagerly concoct tasty jellies
    taste no baffles
For toast, muffins bagels pancakes or waffles

When orchards yield bountifully for the season
Grower consumer picker happy for a reason

by Dalward J DeBruzzi

My Regret

By stupidity is pride and ego increased
They who assume the most know the least

When ages later revelation reveals this
    misguided notion
By then damage, bruised feelings, bruised
    relationships in motion

No contrition orated or 2nd chance will
    erase the ruin and destruction
On lives, feelings, such massive malfunction

Accepting castigation causes bitter
    conductance
Hardest chore is to recognize own massive
    error with great reluctance

by Dalward J DeBruzzi

My Ship

Oh I am the captain of my tidy trim ship
Upon a tiny pond I sail, but limited only to a short dip

I yearn to sail the vast oceans wide, armed with glowing pride
I must downsize my wheel man then have him at my side

I'm constantly sailing in circles but arrive nowhere as I keep turning round and round
The distance it fails to cover is too embarrassing to put to sound

My ambition is to take my ship a sailing way beyond
For this we must find an outlet from the tiny pond

After animating the wheel man he will guide us to the sea
It's exploration we seek you see

We'll sail the waters as the fair winds blow
We'll brave the gales hurricanes and snow

Crashing through waves, water breaking
 over the prow
As my gallant little ship through the waters
 does plow

Journeys end, the fantasy did too, in
 dissolution
The sojourn was an enthralling, exciting trip
 with no conclusion

I am the captain of a tidy little ship in a
 pond small with imagination plus a
 helpful day dream I sail the seas all

by Dalward J DeBruzzi

My Vicarious Travels

Up into the tallest tree
Who climbed here but little me

Waved at the vast world with both hands
In all the corners of all the lands

Saw snow, glaciers, dunes of sand
Animals, clawed, horned, taloned on water
and on land

The people, yellow, white, black, and red
All colors with one quest in mind
Seek, find, feed, beings of their own kind

by Dalward J DeBruzzi

Our Ole Farm

I was fourteen when dad sold our ole farm home
Spent many happy interesting years
working playing in fields content to roam

Grew own vegetables, beef, pork chickens too
The life was hard but satisfying for true

Grew up with siblings in happy family of five
All healthy content we all did thrive

Many years later felt nostalgic recalling days gone by
Drifted out that way thought I'd give it a try

Headed up the old dusty road, weed covered
Abandoned, windowless house in shambles and disrepair
House forlorn rotting haven for animals to share

Delighted seeing old rusted plow, rotting bridle of leather
The Ole Farm now looking smaller decayed from weather

Now only a fading memory of a once working farm
Abandoned but still retaining its nostalgic charm

by Dalward J DeBruzzi

Parting

I put no further claim upon your young heart
I lament trembling it appears were drifting
    apart

We refrained from speaking of hopes we
    must flee to avoid stagnation
Our common thought no future hope can
    cause restoration

Oh what words can dispel the fears when
    from twined hearts thee must sever
Needing to part for ever

Tho years since we parted can na'er be
    undone
At unguarded moments my mind is bestirred
    anon

I remember as yesterday the final separation
You turned at the bottom of the stair gave a
    tearful leisurely valedictory wave then
    abstraction

Contemporary American Poetry – 78 New Poems

Years have marched on the parting never
I sit at times dreaming before the sever

by Dalward J DeBruzzi

Porky Piggi

My name is Porky Piggi live in a sty
It's muddy filthy, couldn't keep clean if I try

Slushy, oozing, I'm all covered with splattered grime
Lolling in muck delights me just fine

People come by gawk, insulting with a sneer and jeers
My feelings bruised reduce me to tears

When full grown got treated right
Sprayed me clean took me on a ride
Strangers looked me over said I gave them pride

Woke up in Schultz'es Butcher Shop to oral praise
Everyone wanting me I was the current craze

I traveled all over as chops, pork loins or
bacon
Making customers happy nothing was
untaken

If being wanted and popular got me this end
I'll settle for a sty and the slushy mud my
friend

by Dalward J DeBruzzi

Potent Love

I hit rock bottom was very blue
Met a lovely maiden, despondent too

Expressed sorrow, regret, a second attempt at failed domesticity
We comforted each other with therapeutic consistency

She was a savior, my guiding star to avoid regression
No longer missed the tables, cards, dice for their possession

She basked in my company, care, and protection
We gave completion, love and support to each other avoiding separation

Love is not vain, jealous, plebian or deficient in affinity
It's willingness caring of others, devoted with dignity

Love dissipates despair when bitter caustic
and blue
It rescued both my lovely maiden,
resurrected me too

by Dalward J DeBruzzi

Profound Thought

Common sense is not always too common in this day
Not utilized with frequency it's sad to say

Judgment requires thought sometimes not engaged
Those who use it benefit to arrive at decisions of sage

The torturous path from birth to demise
Provides highs and lows and much surprise

I'm not a spokesman or oracle for the dead
But most will tell you they died unread

Majority failed to reach maximum breadth of potential
Massive ubiquitous flaw on worldly masses unintentional

by Dalward J DeBruzzi

Proposal

The beauties of lilacs, roses all flora are
  quite divine
But exceeding by far to this pinning heart of
  mine

Is a face of perfection and tis thine
It makes day brighter, happier, you are my
  shrine

In the vast array of tender terms with your
  charm and grace
None exceeds your exquisite form and face

Oh sweet beauteous maiden capturer of my
  love and life
On bended knee I ask your blessing and be
  my wife

by Dalward J DeBruzzi

Contemporary American Poetry – 78 New Poems

Redemption

The man who has cleansed his hands of
>tainted life will have a new start
A recital from deep within his heart

When escape or avoidance is unavoidable a
>man must provide resistance
Grasp a weapon firmly in his hand then
>desist with persistence

The world will not remain motionless for
>anyone even not for me or you
Don't count solely on wealth to sustain and
>see you through

Countless bodies lie in the burial ground
Their feeling existence was found

All ends are the same do well do good when
>no morrow
Laments and approval will be sincere with
>sorrow

by Dalward J DeBruzzi

Relentless

Rain falls on grass, trees and me
Over flows rivers, swamps ships at sea

Then evaporates, condensates, precipitates again
On dry fields and crops needed when

Floods dams, river banks, levees, wreaks destruction
Causing a mold introduction
Bridges gone, levees awash drives people away from home

Range far and wide to identify the culprit to blame
Look no further mother nature must bear the shame

by Dalward J DeBruzzi

Relit

Even though you waved a final sign of
 goodbye
My passion not cooled shed tears till dry

Confused what happened why you wanted
 to let it die
Failed to make sense all logic did defy

I remembered our first kiss and all that
 came after
With those good times and continuous
 laughter

Crushed, disappointed with complete
 rejection
I sit and mope, brood, pining to regain your
 affection

After months of consistent prayers my door
 bell ringing
She was standing there a dreamy sigh me
 tingling
We resumed our love without explanation of
 any kind

With neither one resistant
Did our chemistry prevail or was psyche
    aura consistent

If so prayers were answered as the solution
    to a confused heart string
New credibility to prayers seems advisable
    thing

by Dalward J DeBruzzi

River of Life

See yon glittering waves in impish play
Cleanses the banks pilfers the flowers away

In full bloom and prime beauty they perish
When displaying reds, yellows blues sublime
    beauty to cherish

The swift Mississippi surrounds swiftly
    moving cargo steamers
Hurrying them downstream with goods,
    produce life giving tonnage to persons
    dependent, leaners

Churning roiling waters eddying astern as
    they skim
Along past youth hugging shores on rafts
Generalously propelling all other rivercrafts

Forceful current mighty and strong carrying
    cargo and goods like a main artery to
    towns hamlets even a metropolis
Failing to provide water and sewage
    removal would cause a necropolis

From Lake Itasca in Northern Minnesota to Gulf of Mexico way the mighty Miss gives nourishment
Never ceases bright hopeful encouragement

260 varieties of fish sixty types of mussels
The river toils night and day in silent active tussles

The mighty Miss persistent unstoppable an aura of nobility
Dependable hardly expendable devoted with reliability

The mighty Miss persistent dutiful in productibility depositing rich fertile loam along banks with soil
Asking no thanks, for its steady daily toil

by Dalward J DeBruzzi

Sanctified

Only unblessed ones never to have rapture
    complete
Would inquire of our feelings and ask why
    it's so sweet

Do atoms rotate and spin do they exist but
    unseen
Even those feeling rapture are unable to
    come clean

Efforts to define it are confined to a smile,
    sigh or a look sweet
Its illusivisity is diaphanous and intangible
    but yet real as a heart beat

Any fortuitous romantic lucky enough to
    have gloried in its splendor can feel
    anointed and blessed
For a special gift was bestowed you having
    been psychically possessed

by Dalward J DeBruzzi

Secret Trips

From early morn all day through
I play amicably with my friends true

But every night when my eyes close tight
I enter a mystic paradise of twinkling stars bright

I visit exotic places on my magic carpet or rocket ship
Tahiti, pyramids, Paris, Alps all in one trip

My selection is varied, vast with expectations
My travels surfeit with animated locations

Awaking is pleasing when recounting my dreams
My private secrets protect my wild imaginative extremes

On the morrow, spend a normal day no vary
Anxiously waiting for bedtime again to plan itinerary

by Dalward J DeBruzzi

Shades of Lilacs

Tiny lovely tinted shades of lavender
    flowers of beauty
A worthy added adornment to any cutey

Possesses stunning loveliness of aesthetic
    bloom
Emanating perfumed scents flooding oe'r
    the room

With lolling languishing gaze a torpid
    drowse yields
Tender warm sensations ere flowered fields

Lilac creations floral candidates admired for
    breathtaking panorama of splendor
Never failing creation of beauteous engender

So striking one suspects heavenly
    intervention
Did the god Flora decree the Lilac "QUEEN
    of FLOWERS" with predictive
    intention?

Contemporary American Poetry – 78 New Poems

If so startling blazing beauty fulfills the prophecy with perfection

by Dalward J DeBruzzi

Song Writers

Is there a song with voice if there is no ear
    to hear the tone
Or if unable to taste the sweetness or dispel
    a strident moan

Some writers thirst for fame as others gasp
    for air
Living between anonymity and insecurity a
    constant dare

Surviving by means thin and narrow until
    hopeful success
What is deeply yearned may never occur no
    promise yet must endure duress

One over cast day sun burst through with
    brilliant rays song spurted up in charts
    gained me fame and fortune to stay
If you wish hopefully, believe in yourself
    ardently and pray faithfully you may
    win the fray

by Dalward J DeBruzzi

Spells and Curses

On a dark moonless threatening Halloween night
Wind was howling the night a shrieking fright

Cackling wrinkled toothless witches grouped conjuring venomous potions by design
Malignantly eager to administer to victims by design

Crowded around swirling bubbling rising tendrils from boiling cauldron
Day after Halloween witches pointed fingers at each other in commotion
Affixing blame for poor batch of failed impotent spell binding potion

Contest of good and evil rages here and there high and low
Even on Halloween casualties will show

Wisps and vapors from my eyes did not shroud The evidence of perpetual battle of the dark side and the proud

by Dalward J DeBruzzi

The Ace

Deception, deceiving, misleading is in
    disrepute, in application
To a pitcher it's an art form of artistic
    selection

Altering an apparent destination of aim to
    create an illusion
The object a vision for affectation of
    conventional confusion

Avoiding the obvious to a batter the goal,
Must be apparently on target yet not really,
    or will suffer a toll

Skill in optical distortion so batter suffers ill
    fate
Denying batter comprehension until too late
Determines whether or not the pitcher in
    future will become a great

by Dalward J DeBruzzi

The Asian Miracle

Am an Asian you see and am a proud
    American now by the book
People treat me well, respect my different
    look

I follow the laws, answer questions when
    police stop me
Have never been to jail, never a party to a
    riot, questionable protests is not for
    me you see

We Asians work hard get educated many in
    professions
We far exceed many Americans in progress,
    quality of life avoiding undesirable
    obsessions

Generations of people who have been here
    long past
Still unassimilated or fully accepted

Maybe their mode of behavior or priorities of practice
Should be revised become compliant, affable interactive

I studied the history, the evolution of demographics
I am pleased we Asians are few in prisons as we obey the law

by Dalward J DeBruzzi

The Dream

Millions of people in most countries in world
    have one repetitive compelling dream
How can I emigrate to America my recurring
    theme

Dense population refugee camps threat to
    life by warfare
From civil wars terrorists who life means
    not to care

Family people only sin minority faction
    same religion
Nothing religious killing fellow members
    sending them to perdition

What fervent sense of paradise when family
    smiling content nourishment safe
    sleep not in question
This not common frequently found making
    way to USA an obsession

Where stones, trees, homes not bombed away
Emigration to USA still the thought night
 and day

Oh! how can I get to America? still my
 passionate dream
My heightened recurring theme

Fresh water food no bombing or shelling
All I want basic good things Americans
 enjoy find compelling

Oh America make a spot for me it should be
 in the offing
Some USA citizens complain criticize their
 president
If they're so unhappy maybe they will
 establish a precedent

Trade places with my harsh life for their
 bountiful existence

You know their gripe is trivia not sensible or
    sane
Swap with me and discover fine imagined
        dissatisfaction inane
Oh America take me let me not pine in vain

by Dalward J DeBruzzi

Contemporary American Poetry – 78 New Poems

The Eelymosinarry

Wind was blowing hard with icy ferocity
Shivering the old shriveled, tattered man
    suffering atrocity

His numb fingerless gloves fastened on icy
    handles of stolen shopping cart
Tough pushing through snow on way from
    the mart

Picked out old newspapers from street
    waste container thinking bitterly my
    use this better than a letter?
Thoughts clouded, confused doesn't life
    have something better? Like another
    sweater?

His deadened eyes showed bitterness on
    his lined weather beaten face
He turned towards the park behind dense
    bushes found his space

Squeezed in between entered his cardboard box
Reinforced his thin coat with layers of newspapers curled into fetal position like a hibernating fox

Wishing for a great warming fire he chatters his teeth beginning to drop off for survival sleep needed
Must be able to wend between cars in morn as he pleaded
It's not hard to look needy an sorrowful in this type of existence
When it's your true identity not a role or a jest just tepid persistence will do the rest

Its amendments are barren, distasteful at best
When your main thought is no disturbance if survival fails the test

Morn old man up goes to work to pander price for breakfast morn begs his coins walks between cars feeling a joy as elated as a twinkling star

**Walks in for breakfast with a voice of good cheer
Orders "two shots and a beer."**

by Dalward J DeBruzzi

The Ferryboat

Take me across in your boat with water so
    deep
Must cross to get home to get some sleep

My purse is full can pay toll for my passage
    and wares
No alternative unless travel long way
    without cares

Current is swift strong not perilous
Not a subject for querulous

Five cents for passengers same for freight
Ferrryman with long poll casts off no wish
    to be late

by Dalward J DeBruzzi

The Order of Life

I know I never amounted to very much
Even now don't think I ever will as such

There are many like me, in last days, old on hold resigned to fate
Limited, restricted, slowed down, waiting with calm resignation for the final date

What can we do to grasp some joy in this gloomy time
Can you get something for nothing? Is it a crime?

Is there guilt to feel blue? When everything has passed you by
Children don't come, sick, alone in a lonely room, just cry

Then you remember it could have been worse
An empty purse, a shortened life, incarceration a curse

Though end is certain to be lonely unsung, unpleaded
No grief for me please, it's not needed

I raised two kids free of drink or a drug,
My deserted demise I simply dismiss with a shrug

Children never regret forgetting their parents' sacrifices
Until old themselves then realize their negligent sins, vices

by Dalward J DeBruzzi

The Panacea for All Ills

In life we strive for peace with placidity
Seldom gaining the status, the culprit cupidity

Material drives erode judgment, morality
Relentless desire present as nearing release approaches finality

Death is growing shadows and darkness grows, much more not in vain
Cessation of troubles, release of stress, elimination of all pain

Death is a friend, a haven for the weary, sick, disillusioned, defeated, dreary
A sanctuary for escape for mortals with ponderous burdens their distress now deleted

Death in normal chronological succession is a friend to look forward too
It's a scalpel of mercy incising all pain is benevolent and merciful with thankful cosmic milieu

by Dalward J DeBruzzi

The Rose

The rose is a plant or flower to some
To millions world over there's much more,
 much more to come

Since times eternal presence the Rose is
 cast by universal early decree a
 special legacy
Sharing vertiginous scents with gods in
 amorous efficacy

Baker, butcher, banker, barber, some of
 countless many using the Rose to
 convey the emotional message
"Will you be my valentine" my heart to thine

by Dalward J DeBruzzi

Unrealistic

I was healthy, wealthy and not very
    handsome see
Delusion a young, fresh beauty fell in love
    with me

We were married a year then I shed a tear
Proclaimed no longer loved me I fear

Then the brutal evidence she never did
I was victim of deception, subterfuge,
    subtle chicanery
A dupe of refined slick quackery

No marriage contract was signed for
    protection woe is me now, half as
    wealthy, unhealthy to boot, broken
    hearted
A fool and his money is soon parted

by Dalward J DeBruzzi

Unseen Companion

Whenever children play, are never really alone,
Though appear solitary, have an unseen companion unknown

If children are happy but lonely and good
A playmate companion emerges and should

He is not seen, a picture undrawn
But assured he is present here, there, everywhere

When good children play solo are, content, happy,
Can tell you why?
It's the unseen companion whose standing near by

by Dalward J DeBruzzi

Unsung Brave Women

Great offering of these women with maternity
Under arduous survival they commit to it
   with firmity

Yawning vast space existence lonely and
   boring
On the thinly populated prairie no social
   touring

Harshest of all on pioneer wives isolated no
   contact with humans despondent
   depressed
Full condemnation unblessed

Few fail to cope unfitted for solitary life
   strict undeserved quarantine
   demoralized mentally affected
Some gone mad, defying reason excessively
   beyond realm of sad but most endured
   and disaffected

Silence is golden a fine adage at times
In sparse populated areas and eschewing
    crime

Plucky strong pioneer women helped settle
    the West
Were courageous strong resourceful
    enduring among the finest the best

by Dalward J DeBruzzi

Vulnerable

A small white cottage happy man and wife
Sunshine warmth contentment with life

Constantly thanking providence for their paradise
Peace, mutual sharing, trust, no unwelcome surprise

She tends to him and he to her
Doing for each other secret to rapport

Accepting duties willingly and equally we concur
Is vital to cohesive union no need to seek succor

The seasons come the seasons go
The geese fly South annually we know

Winter time brings fluffy snow
Days shorten, equinox, then the cycle begins again we know

Most things ethereal, passing through phases with strife
Except happy man and wife in small white cottage
Immune to change no alteration in their dotage

by Dalward J DeBruzzi

Was Abortion the Right Thing?

What would he be like if I let him live and be born?
The abortion was timely convenient a life shorn

Merlin a guru a sage with psychic assistance
Chronicled the panorama with meticulous persistence

Infancy a delight babe chortled cooed never ill colic or demanding
Felt the sting and the loss of a precious desirous tot
Questioned the wisdom of the abortion a lot

Teen life a debacle in reverse thievery, robbery incarceration with frequency
Plethora of heartbreak, drugs, besotted no leniency

Great despair no regret abortion did occur
I spared him misery a life dismal an evil blur

Contemporary American Poetry – 78 New Poems

I took a life yes a gigantic crime accept the guilt
Feel exonerated to avoid further milk spilt

by Dalward J DeBruzzi

What Did I Do?

I grabbed my inheritance frittered it away
With foolish prodigality reckless display

On lustful, debauching orgiastic existence
I lost my mind, with little resistance

My addiction was fatal, thorough, quite complete
Destitute, wealth dissipated, health eroded a major defeat

I now sleep in alleys, underpasses, gangways, park bench a treat
Scrounging for morsels in garbage cans, begging for coins to get something to eat

Industriousness, pecuniosity with prudence as guides
Is new direction as uncontrollable crave subsides

Contemporary American Poetry – 78 New Poems

**It's less exciting, but the right direction for me
I'm climbing back up from the gutter you see**

by Dalward J DeBruzzi

What Is Love?

To love her is to belie tainted romance
She's neither mine nor yours though enamored

For us there is slim, slender chance
She's a bright lamp attracting moths oh! romance! delectable trance,

Wish to hold her in tender embrace ever to be excited
Entwined in intimate contact pleas recited

No one is her favorite she wants not, cares not, withdrawn far, far away in her esoteric domain of whimsicality
When devoted, affection is absent, the unfulfilled one suffers inhumanity

Who can chart the course in love of every diverted scheme
With fortuity, hope and prayer some may gain their dream

Contemporary American Poetry – 78 New Poems

I won no maiden, I cherished to have for my own
Went on a spree reckless, with wild oats sown

After natural recovery, stumbled on to discovery from time tested lore
There is a plethora of women for every man just be vigilant, perceptive, intensive, look some more

by Dalward J DeBruzzi

What Next

Sometimes winds come from the west
At times it's the worst or maybe the best

From the east might be unfit for man nor beast
Weather capricious for farmers could be famine or feast

From north cold blasts icy sleet or snow
Even mild at times you never really know

by Dalward J DeBruzzi

Contemporary American Poetry – 78 New Poems

What's a Friend?

Some people are disappointing some are devotedly true
Who is who is up to you

Some people do you good some do not
Few will even do you harm when they appear to do a lot

It's hard to identify the frauds from the sincere
Time reveals the reliable one we can cheer

They answer your call when desperately needed
Your feeling elated when your call for succor heeded

Charlatan posing as friend waiting to aid
By never stepping up whatever the cause exposes themselves as a pretender to fade

by Dalward J DeBruzzi

What's in a Name?

A misanthropic vengeful, noxious archfiend
echoed
From profound depths below

Gloated with rapturous glee, celebrating my
forlorn misery feeling low,
His motivation, to feel triumphant, and crow
and glow

His name is varied, deceiver, fallen angel,
Satan, dragon, evil and more
Any name dour unclean, foreboding will be
fine for sure

Sinner, tempter all his names to spread
horrific plague
Obstructs, defies God, through
vulnerabilities vague

Seeing me lose my sole life's love pleases, sates his
Appetite for malignancy and pain
Unless he sees hurt, misery his disappointment is present denying him pleasures now in vain

Tragedy, suffering delights him like fine spirits and foods
His day optimum when able to prevent good moods

He does not deny his subtle infiltration says were partners in the struggling contest
Acting alone he's ineffective innocuous at best

You can protect yourself by standing fast and firm
With spiritual help he will be stymied and defeated in turn

by Dalward J DeBruzzi

Wisdom

Molly was merry on way to market with
    cheese
She had worked and toiled to have wares to
    please
Buy cloth from Gimber's store make dresses
    a breeze

With money from dresses buy bonnets,
    trinkets and shoes and of finery the
    best
When appear in town young men will pursue
    with zest

Lost in thought of glorious reward she
    loosened her grip on her cheese
    treasure
It slipped and fell snatched by wolf in mid
    air with pleasure

Contemporary American Poetry – 78 New Poems

She related her story to mother at home
   wisely said
These words of wisdom have oft been read

But only rarely have they been matched
"Never count chickens before they are
   hatched"

by Dalward J DeBruzzi

Women

Let's not cast stones though some women
    are lewd
Unfair to condemn their activities as totally
    eschewed

Although at times their behavior offends
Their mere sex tends to make amends

It's charitable to allow them straying from
    conventionality
Women are needed it's biological rationality

Lest how will propagation continue to
    increase population
All women even those with imperfections
    engage in copulation

Which is the function purpose and duty of
    women
Let's appreciate women fulfilling their
    destination

by Dalward J DeBruzzi

Would This Last?

My live in girlfriend says she loves me so
With all my heart this I know

My heart is in angst when she's not close by
Enduring her absence is hard but I try

She pleads wedding, now is the thing to do
I think to do that would be wonderful too

But a huge obstacle denies this connubial bliss
We both have the drive and desire but age amiss

We're unable to thwart bodily changes that surely do come on
She is forty-three, I am eighty one

by Dalward J DeBruzzi

CPSIA information can be obtained
at www.ICGtesting.com
Printed in the USA
FFOW04n0223010418
46123021-47176FF